SPIRIT OF THE
WELSH
MOUNTAIN
PONY

FLEUR HALLAM

First published in Great Britain in 2010

British Library Cataloguing-in-Publication Data
A CIP record for this title is available from the British Library

ISBN 978 0 85710 029 0

PiXZ Books
Halsgrove House, Ryelands Industrial Estate,
Bagley Road, Wellington, Somerset TA21 9PZ
Tel: 01823 653777
Fax: 01823 216796
email: sales@halsgrove.com

An imprint of Halstar Ltd,
part of the Halsgrove group of companies
Information on all Halsgrove titles
is available at: www.halsgrove.com

Printed and bound in China by Toppan Leefung Printing Ltd

Introduction

I have been involved with native ponies of the British Isles since my childhood. They are all a unique part of Britain's history and heritage. The Welsh Mountain pony, or Section A of the Welsh Stud Book, is one of the most beautiful, hardy, and elegant of the small Mountain and Moorland breeds. Today these ponies can be found worldwide, and are extremely popular, not just because of their good looks and charming characters, but because they are very versatile and excel in many disciplines, from carriage driving, jumping, and riding, through to being an ideal family pony.

This old breed of mountain pony has roamed the hills and wild moors of Wales for centuries. They should be spirited and pony-like in general character. The ponies have a maximum height of 12hh, and come in a range of colours except piebald or skewbald. They have small pretty heads, the silhouette appearing dished, but never too straight, with bold bright eyes and small pointed ears. The neck should be of good length, with shoulders sloping back to a clearly defined wither. The limbs are set square with good flat bone, and strong round hooves. The tail is set high and carried proudly. Their action is quick, free and straight, knees and hocks well flexed, covering the ground with power. They are small but mighty in appearance and though naturally beautiful they combine great intelligence with the legendary Welsh temperament.

Keen to continue my passion for the British Mountain and Moorland breeds, I have endeavoured to capture the Welsh Mountain ponies in their picturesque native homeland of Wales, from up high on the mountains and hills to the lowlands, through to showing their grace and power on the show field.

A show-winning turnout. Penllyn Plover carries her jockey to
first place in a ridden lead rein class at Cothi Bridge Show 2009.

Opposite page:
Below the boughs of a tree, grey mare Bryndansi Muffin,
a mother of show winners, stands with her foal.

Desiring mother's attention, Bedolfa Angels Passing with her foal.

An evening portrait of mare Glebedale Sensation and friends.

Feminine beauty, portrait of mare Gurnos Eira.

Opposite page:
Radiant at seventeen-years-old, broodmare Bryngwenlli Elen grazes with her colt foal.

A proven broodmare,
and still striking at
twenty-six years,
Bryndansi Melog
with her foal.

Opposite page:
As the evening light
fades over the Tywi
Valley, mares and their
foals of the Hope Stud
catch the last sun rays
of the day.

A classical stance, filly Nantfforchog Blue Velvet.

The charm of youth, bay roan yearling filly Synod Maria.

Left:
Mares and foals of the Nantfforchog Stud are truly at home on their mountainside.

Right:
The warm glow of evening sunlight highlights the prettiness of Polaris Ulissa.

Two Ceulan colt foals, Supersonic and Hamish,
enjoy their youthful playing amongst the buttercups.

An alert pose,
the beautiful grey
mare Rhydyfelin
Silver Leaf.

Smart young stallion Penplas Glyndwr at the home of Bryngwenlli.

Eye-catching in the evening sunlight, Pwlle Adell with her foal.

Standing proud, chestnut roan filly Ceulan Mia, a daughter of Royal Welsh Champion 2007 Frongoch Cardi.

Filly foal Islyn Hufen has a doze in the warmth of spring.

Filly Porthmawr Niwl y Bore, winner of the three year old
filly or gelding class at Cothi Bridge Show 2009.

Gurnos Narina enjoys a cooling breeze on a warm summer's day.

On their natural hillside environment, mare Gurnos Bluebell with her foal Gurnos Zodiac.

Generations – broodmare Lacy Heather Bee, mother to one
of the foals, grandmother to two, and an aunt to the fourth foal.

Friars Queen of Hearts patiently waits in line, before taking first prize in her class, and Welsh Section A Champion at the Cothi Bridge Show 2009.

Showing his paces, stallion Hope Burns trots out at Cothi Bridge Show during his class.

Sweetness and innocence of two cheeky Glebedale colt foals.

A pretty pair, Ceulan Libby with her five week old filly foal Ceulan Lilly.

Delightful cheekiness, colt Glebedale Mumbo Jumbo peers over a gate.

Opposite page:
Pregnancy can be tiring! Nineteen-year-old broodmare Hope Saphier heavily in foal.

Good all-rounder, Blackoak Jon with her young jockey and handler.

Opposite page:
Shimmering lake waters behind,
Lacy Heather Bee peacefully grazes.

A chestnut gentleman, stallion Blaenau Finlay.

Sure-footed over all terrain, roan mare Gurnos Dreamer leads the way.

A line of ladies,
with Bedolfa Agnes
in the middle.

Three-year-old colt Weston Distinction stands smartly for the judge,
and takes the first prize in his class at Cothi Bridge Show 2009.

Polaris Fairy Charm and her resting colt foal Pentyrch Newman, both enjoy the warmth of a sunny day.

An elegant lead rein turnout, Dijkzicht Boris with his
small jockey and handler stand for the judge.

The purity of youth, foal
Gurnos Tribulation.

Opposite page:
Beautiful grey ladies graze
contentedly with their foals
at the Glebedale Stud.

A group of three-year-olds at Gurnos Farm, X factor, Leona, and Pixar.

Opposite page:
Contrast of colours, Hope Miss Amber with her foal both gleam in the evening sunlight.

Filly Bryngwenlli Mari shows
her ground-covering trot over
natural terrain.

Proud mother Pentyrch Zena feeds her foal
Pentyrch Nicole.

Opposite page:
Beautiful grey dapples – Hope Dafney, a filly by Gartnonnel Snapdragon.

Grey stallion Criccieth Frydyn takes his herd back up the mountain.

A bay beauty, Gurnos Alicia.

Glebedale Armani with her foal happily at home on a working farm.

Gurnos Mystery relieves an itch while her foal sleeps peacefully.

Watching over his domain, handsome stallion Pentyrch Ivor in Whitelodge field.

Opposite page:
An evening stroll round the hill top. Some of the Hope Stud's mares and foals.

Gurnos Nutmeg grazes on a hillside, whilst her foal finds
the ideal position to have a suckle from his mother.

Standing to attention, a line up of pretty Hope Stud mares with their foals.

Motherly pride. Islyn Hyder feeds her filly
foal Islyn Hufen amongst the bluebells.

Menai Angel Aur and Bryngwenlli
Elin Jones are shown off to their best
at Cothi Bridge Show.

Opposite page:
Freedom. Bryngwenlli Mari with the Cambrian Hills in the background.

Bedolfa Allt Goch living naturally with
the herd on the Black Mountains.

Foal Gurnos First Kiss with mares
Gurnos Last Dance and Maescwm Disipline
on Merthyr Common.

Opposite page:
Watching yard activities over her stable door, the pretty filly Pentyrch Katrina.

A hill with a view. Pwlle Awella with the Tywi Valley in the background.

Opposite page: Peeking over mother's mane, filly foal Pergwm Katie.

Islyn Asbri peers over a stone wall at a neighbour.

Naturally beautiful, mare Nantfforchog Seren-Y-Nos.

Islyn Modlan grazes happily keeping a watchful eye on her resting foal.

Mild flirtation between grey mare Polaris Isis with stallion Phildon Chief.

59

Islyn Ania stands besides the shores of Trawsfynydd Lake.

Left:
An inquisitive young foal,
Bryngwenlli Eryr Du.

Stallion Gurnos Soundtrack watches over his herd on Merthyr Common.

Contended foal Gurnos Pot of Gold relaxes in
a patch of sunlight, with dam Gurnos Silvia.

Opposite page:
Curiosity. The attention of some of the Hope Stud's broodmares is caught.

Follow me. Three-week-old filly foal Ceulan Carol follows her dam Ceulan Cariad.